WORDS OF EXPRESSION

WRITTEN BY

COLIN BOYNTON

ISBN : 978-1-9162837-1-8

COPYRIGHT : COLIN BOYNTON 2021

INDEX

1. THINGS
2. PAUSE FOR THOUGHT
3. ANOTHER WHY
4. GETTING OLDER
5. A HOLE IN ONE!
6. EAR, EAR…
7. TOO FAST
8. GOODBYE
9. COMING BACK
10. THERE BUT FOR THE GRACE…
11. PEOPLE
12. LOVING ARMS
13. WELL I NEVER!
14. TRY…
15. SALES AGAIN…
16. FAITH, HOPE, CHARITY
17. SOME PEOPLE
18. THE PEOPLE SHOW
19. TIME OF MEMORIES
20. IN A MODERN WORLD - 1
21. WEATHER THE CHANGE
22. IN A MODERN WORLD - 2
23. BLACK AND WHITE
24. LAST IN LINE
25. BARGAIN HUNTERS

26. MOONLIGHT
27. SINGING A SONG
28. THE LONG GOODBYE
29. A SIGN OF THE TIMES
30. NO REGRETS
31. CARE HOME BLUES
32. AND AFTER…
33. DEAR FRIEND
34. TOGETHER – FOREVER - AMEN
35. THE MAN HIMSELF
36. IS THAT ALL WE DO?
37. THE END
38. SILENCE IS GOLDEN
39. ME, ME, ME
40. THROUGH IT ALL…
41. REALITY CHECK
42. THROUGH STORMS OF TROUBLED TIMES
43. HAPPY!
44. A LESSON IN LIFE
45. RUNNING AWAY?
46. TEDDY BEAR LOVE
47. IMMORTALITY?
48. WAITING…?
49. HISTORY LESSON
50. WOULD I…?

51. DOGGIE LOVE
52. FAILING MEMORY - 1
53. PASSING BY
54. COVID 19 2020
55. THE GAME
56. THE ROSE
57. SOLITARY
58. PRESENT DAY LIVING
59. SOMETHING STRANGE
60. UNCERTAIN OF THE CERTAIN
61. DOGGIE LOVE - 2
62. TREES
63. STONES
64. WATER
65. DEJA - VU
66. COUNTING
67. ONLY THE LONELY
68. JUST A DREAMER?
69. MOVING ON…
70. IN MEMORIAM
71. REALLY THERE ?
72. THE JOURNEY
73. A CRY IN THE DARK
74. HIDDEN FROM VIEW
75. WHEN YOU'RE SMILING

1. THINGS

DON'T LOOK TOO DEEP
OR YOU MIGHT FIND
SOMETHING HIDDEN
IN MY MIND
THINGS IN THERE
THAT MIGHT SURPRISE
HIDDEN DEEP
BEHIND MY EYES
THINGS YOU MIGHT NOT WANT TO SEE
WAITING THERE
TO JUST BREAK FREE

DON'T LOOK TOO DEEP
OR QUESTION ME
THERE'S THINGS INSIDE
THAT SHOULD NOT BE
THINGS INSIDE
I CAN'T ESCAPE
I CAN'T AVOID
THEIR FORM AND SHAPE
THINGS YOU MIGHT NOT WANT TO SEE
WAITING THERE
TO BE SET FREE

DON'T LOOK TOO DEEP
DON'T LOOK AT ALL
AS I BUILD UP
MYSELF A WALL
TO KEEP ME SAFE
BOTH NIGHT AND DAY
NOT HEARING WHAT
YOU HAVE TO SAY
THERE'S THINGS YOU MIGHT NOT WANT TO SEE
HIDDEN THERE
SO DEEP IN ME.

2. PAUSE FOR THOUGHT.

DID NO ONE EVER TELL YOU
THAT EVEN ANGELS CRY
BUT YOU WILL NEVER SEE ONE
WITH A TEARDROP IN THEIR EYE
THEY ALWAYS HIDE THEM FROM US
SO WE DON'T EVEN SEE
THAT ANGELS ARE NO DIFFERENT
FROM EITHER YOU OR ME
THEY SPEND THEIR TIME PROTECTING
THE LIKES OF ME AND YOU
BUT SOMETIMES SOMEONE CAN'T BE HELPED
THERE'S NOTHING THEY CAN DO
THAT'S WHEN ANGELS SHED A TEAR
BUT THEN THEY CARRY ON
DOING ALL THE WORK THEY CAN
THEIR JOB IS NEVER DONE

DID NO ONE EVER TELL YOU
THAT EVEN ANGELS CRY
IT'S OFTEN SOMETHING HUMANS DO
BRINGS TEARDROPS TO THEIR EYE
WHEN THEY SEE THE MESS WE MAKE
THE DAMAGE THAT WE DO
AN ANGEL'S WORK IS HARDER
BECAUSE OF ME AND YOU
THEY WANT TO TEACH US ALL RESPECT
AND TRY TO TEACH US LOVE
BUT NO ONE LISTENS TO THE VOICE
CALLING FROM ABOVE
AND WHEN AN ANGEL SHEDS A TEAR
NO MATTER HOW THEY TRY
WE NEVER LISTEN TO THEM
NO WONDER ANGELS CRY

3. ANOTHER WHY

WHY CAN THE WORLD
BE A HORRIBLE PLACE
YET I GO AROUND
WITH SMILES ON MY FACE?
WHY DO WE KILL
AND WHY DO WE MAIM
WHEN I STILL HAVE LOVE
AS MY MIDDLE NAME?
WHY DO WE DO
SOME THINGS THAT WE DO
AND YET CARRY ON
LIKE NOBODY KNEW?
WHY ARE WE BLIND
TO THINGS THAT WE SEE
WE LET THEM GO ON
AND JUST LET THEM BE?
WHY ARE WE DEAF
TO CRIES THAT WE HEAR
WHAT DO WE LACK
AND WHAT DO WE FEAR?
WHY DO I HURT
AND WHY DO I GRIEVE
WHEN I KNOW WHAT I KNOW
AND I STILL BELIEVE?

4. GETTING OLDER

WITH THE YEARS JUST PASSING BY
THE OLDER THAT WE GET
THERE SEEMS TO BE MUCH MORE WE LEARN
WITH MUCH MORE TO FORGET.
THE ACHES WE GET KEEP MOUNTING
AND QUICKLY WE SLOW DOWN
AND WRINKLES STAY ACROSS OUR BROW
EVERY TIME WE FROWN.
WE CANNOT DO THE THINGS WE DID
NO MATTER HOW WE TRY
AND YET WE'LL KEEP ON GOING
AS YEARS KEEP PASSING BY.

WE'LL LIVE OUR LIVES WITH MEMORIES
BUT SOME THEY WILL FORGET
AND LIVE THEIR LIVES QUITE UNAWARE
AND HAVING NO REGRET.
OUR HAIR MAY TURN TO SILVER
OUR TEETH MAY ALL FALL OUT
OUR EYESIGHT MAY NOT BE AS GOOD
WE'LL SHUFFLE ALL ABOUT.
WE'LL STRUGGLE WITH SOME THINGS WE DO
SOME THINGS WE'LL DO WITH EASE
WE'LL SPEND OR DAYS REMEMBERING
OUR LIVES WITH MEMORIES.

5. A HOLE IN ONE!

THE STRANGEST THING JUST HAPPENED
ON MY WAY TODAY
I WASN'T GOING TO TELL YOU
BUT I THOUGHT THAT I SHOULD SAY
I FELL IN TO A POTHOLE
IN THE MIDDLE OF THE ROAD
JUST AS I WAS CROSSING
CARRYING MY LOAD
I DROPPED MY BAGS WHILE FALLING
AND SCUFFED MY LEFT HAND SHOE
STRUGGLED TO GET UP AGAIN
DIDN'T KNOW WHAT TO DO
I CRIED OUT AND I CALLED OUT
BUT NO ONE HEARD MY PLEA
I LAY THERE IN THAT POTHOLE
AND NO ONE SEEMED TO SEE
THEY WALKED AROUND AND STRODE ACROSS
AND STILL THEY PASSED ME BY
THEY DIDN'T SEE ME LYING THERE
AND DIDN'T HEAR MY CRY
THE RAIN HAD STARTED FALLING
AND I WAS GETTING WET
STILL I STRUGGLED IN THE HOLE
HOW HARD COULD THIS GET?

A HOLE IN ONE! (Cont)

JUST AS I WAS GIVING UP
THE HOPE OF CLIMBING FREE
I ROLLED ON TO MY KNEES ONCE MORE
THAT'S WHEN I COULD SEE
THE HOLE WAS VERY SHALLOW
I JUST HAD TO STAND
I DIDN'T NEED TO GET SOME HELP
I DIDN'T NEED A HAND
PANIC OVER, FEELING DAFT
I HOPED THAT NO ONE SAW
THE OLD FOOL THAT I FELT I WAS
ROLLING ON THE FLOOR
BUT AS I STARTED WALKING
I HEARD A MIGHTY CHEER
FROM PEOPLE THAT I KNEW QUITE WELL
STANDING VERY NEAR
I BRACED MYSELF WITH HEAD HELD HIGH
AND GENTLY GAVE A WAVE
WALKED ALONG MY WAY BACK HOME
FEELING VERY BRAVE
I DIDN'T LET IT WORRY ME
OR CARE WHAT PEOPLE THOUGHT
THIS IS ME, IT'S WHO I AM
MY FEARS AND WORRIES FOUGHT!

6. EAR, EAR...

SNATCHES OF TALKING
AND WHAT PEOPLE SAY
PASSING ME BY
GOING THEIR WAY
IT NEVER MAKES SENSE
THE THINGS THAT I HEAR
HALF FINISHED SENTENCES
REACHING MY EAR

SOME ON THE PHONE
AND SOME WITH A FRIEND
THE WORDS THAT I HEAR
SEEM NEVER TO END
GIBBERISH BABBLING
SOUNDS OF GOOD CHEER
ALL THIS AND MORE
REACHING MY EAR.

7. TOO FAST…

HERE'S TO THE FUTURE
AND DAYS GONE BY
THE SUN AND THE MOON
AND STARS IN THE SKY
THE HOPES AND THE WISHES
THAT NEVER CAME TRUE
THE DREAMS WE HOLD ON TO
BOTH OLD AND NEW
HERE'S TO THE PAST
THE MEMORIES WE STORE
THE PEOPLE WE KNOW
AND THE ONE'S FROM BEFORE
OUR FRIENDS AND RELATIONS
FROM PRESENT AND PAST
HERE'S TO OUR HAPPINESS
LONG MAY IT LAST
HERE'S TO THE PRESENT
AND THINGS THAT WE DO
PLACES WERE GOING
AND THOSE WE PASS THROUGH
THE THINGS THAT WE'RE SEEING
AND WHAT WE MIGHT SAY
WE'LL JUST GO ON LIVING
OUR LIVES DAY BY DAY.
HERE'S TO THE FUTURE
AND HERE'S TO THE PAST
HERE'S TO THE PRESENT
IT'S ALL GONE TOO FAST.

8. GOODBYE.

GOODBYE IS SUCH A LONELY WORD
SO VERY HARD TO SAY
WHETHER IT'S FOREVER
OR ONLY FOR A DAY
WE THINK WE KNOW IT'S MEANING
AND SAY IT FEELING SAD
WHETHER IT'S FOREVER
OR FOR THE THINGS WE HAD
SOMETIMES IT MEANS AN ENDING
AND HAVING TO LET GO
WHETHER IT'S FOREVER
YOU DO NOT ALWAYS KNOW
SOMETIMES IT'S 'TIL TOMORROW
OR JUST ANOTHER DAY
GOODBYE IS SUCH A LONELY WORD
THAT'S VERY HARD TO SAY

9. COMING BACK.

THERE IS NO ESCAPE
FROM THE TRUTH THAT IS REAL
THERE IS NO ESCAPE
FROM THE FEELINGS WE FEEL
THERE'S NO TURNING BACK
FROM THE FUTURE AHEAD
THERE'S NO TAKING BACK
THE THINGS THAT WE SAID
BE SURE OF YOUR THOUGHTS
THE THINGS THAT YOU SAY
BE SURE OF THE DEEDS
YOU DO EVERY DAY
TRY TO BE KIND
AND TRY TO BE TRUE
FOR WHAT YOU GIVE OUT
WILL COME BACK TO YOU

10. THERE BUT FOR THE GRACE...

THERE'S PEOPLE MUCH WORSE OFF THAN I
SOME SLEEP DOWN ON A STREET
THAT'S WHERE THEY GO TO REST THEIR HEAD
AND BEG FOR FOOD TO EAT.
THERE'S SOMEONE IN A WHEELCHAIR
WHO CANNOT EVEN WALK
SOME WHO CANNOT EVEN SEE
AND SOME WHO CANNOT TALK
THERE'S PEOPLE WHO ARE IN DISTRESS
AFRAID AND SO ALONE
THEY HAVE NO FRIENDS OR FAMILY
THAT THEY CAN CALL THEIR OWN
I KNOW THAT I AM LUCKY
THAT PERSON COULD BE ME
BUT I HAVE GRACE AND FORTUNE
AND LIVE MY LIFE QUITE FREE
AND IF YOU LIVE YOUR LIFE LIKE I
FEW WORRIES AND FEW WOES
GIVE THANKS THE WAY THAT I DO
AND MAKE SURE THAT IT SHOWS

11. PEOPLE

I LIKE TO WATCH THE PEOPLE
PASSING ON THEIR WAY
IF ONLY THEY KNEW WHAT I THOUGHT
SHOULD I REALLY SAY
I LOOK AT WHAT THEY'RE DRESSED IN
THEIR HAIR MIGHT LOOK A MESS
FACES LOOKING TIRED AND WORN
FULL OF LIFE'S DISTRESS
I LISTEN TO THEM TALKING
I WATCH THEM WALKING BY
THEIR EYES ARE TURNED DOWN TO THE GROUND
THEIR HEADS UP IN THE SKY
THEY'RE FULL OF ENTERTAINMENT
AND YET THEY DO NOT KNOW
WHAT I THINK ABOUT THEM
AS ON THEIR WAY THEY GO

12. LOVING ARMS

WRAP YOUR ARMS AROUND A HEART
AND HOLD IT CLOSE AND TIGHT
SHOW IT THAT YOU REALLY CARE
BE THERE BOTH DAY AND NIGHT
THE HEART MAY NOT BE BREAKING
BUT JUST NEED SOMEONE STRONG
IT MAY JUST NEED A LITTLE HUG
BUT NOT FOR VERY LONG
BE KIND AND VERY CARING
BE LOVING AND BE TRUE
OPEN UP YOUR ARMS AND HEART
THAT'S ALL YOU HAVE TO DO

13. WELL I NEVER!

CREATURE OF THE NIGHT
YOU CANNOT CAPTURE ME
I MAY BE IN MY DREAMS
AND CANNOT EVEN SEE
BUT I FEEL YOUR PRESENCE NEAR
YOU'RE MOVING ALL AROUND
BESIDE ME IN THE DARK OF NIGHT
WITHOUT A SINGLE SOUND

CREATURE OF THE NIGHT
YOU WILL NOT FRIGHTEN ME
I FEEL YOUR GENTLE TOUCH
ALTHOUGH I DO NOT SEE
YOU CREEP UP ON MY BED TONIGHT
WHILE I AM HALF ASLEEP
I FEEL YOU CREEP AROUND ME
I WANT TO TAKE A PEEP

CREATURE OF THE NIGHT
I'M SCARED AS I CAN BE
I FEEL STRANGE FEELINGS ALL ABOUT
CLOSING IN ON ME
I WAKE UP WITH A SUDDEN START
AND WONDER WHAT AND WHERE?
TO FIND THE CREATURE OF THE NIGHT
IS JUST MY TEDDY BEAR!

14. TRY…

TRY A SMILE UPON YOUR FACE
TO BRIGHTEN UP A DAY
AND LIGHTEN UP A DARKER WORLD
AS YOU GO YOUR WAY
TRY A LITTLE GENTLE LAUGH
TO RAISE YOUR SPIRITS HIGH
TO MAKE THE WORLD A BRIGHTER PLACE
THAT SHOULDN'T HAVE TO CRY
TRY A LITTLE TENDERNESS
COMPASSIONATE WITH CARE
NO MATTER WHAT IT IS YOU CHOOSE
DON'T BE AFRAID TO SHARE
TRY TO LOVE FROM IN YOUR HEART
SHARE IT ALL ABOUT
THE WORLD COULD BE A BETTER PLACE
OF THAT THERE IS NO DOUBT

15. SALES AGAIN!

OH DEAR THE SALES ARE ON AGAIN
WITH PEOPLE GOING MAD
RUSHING HERE AND RUSHING THERE
IT REALLY IS QUITE SAD
THEY HAVEN'T EVEN TIME TO PAUSE
THERE'S BARGAINS TO BE BOUGHT
EXPRESSIONS THEY HAVE ON THEIR FACE
THEY REALLY ARE QUITE FRAUGHT
HAVE I MISSED A BARGAIN
DID SOMEONE GET THERE FIRST
AND EVEN WITH THE THINGS THEY'VE GOT
THEY STILL HAVE BARGAIN THIRST
SPEND SOME MONEY, SPEND SOME MORE
ON THINGS THEY DO NOT NEED
SALE TIME ALWAYS BRINGS RIGHT OUT
THAT AWFUL THING CALLED GREED.

16. FAITH, HOPE CHARITY

FAITH

NOT EVERYONE'S A WINNER
NOT EVERYONE WILL LOSE
IT ALL DEPENDS ON WHAT YOU DO
AND SOMETIMES WHAT YOU CHOSE
HAVE FAITH IN WHAT YOU'RE DOING
WHO KNOWS WHAT YOU'LL ACHIEVE
HAVE FAITH IN WHERE YOU'RE GOING
AND TRUST WHAT YOU BELIEVE

HOPE

CATCH A STAR THAT'S FALLING
HOLD IT CLOSE AND TIGHT
MAKE A WISH FROM IN YOUR DREAMS
BEFORE THE CLOSE OF NIGHT
FOR DREAMS ARE OFTEN WISHES
AND SOMETIMES DREAMS COME TRUE
BUT CATCHING FALLING STARS IS RARE
AND VERY HARD TO DO
BUT NEVER EVER GIVE UP HOPE
FOR ONE DAY YOU WILL SEE
THAT FALLING STAR UP IN THE SKY
THAT'S MEANT FOR YOU OR ME

CHARITY

GIVE WHAT YOU CAN AND WHEN YOU CAN
BE IT BIG OR SMALL
SOME PEOPLE THEY HAD RICHES
BEFORE THEY TOOK A FALL
WHAT GOES AROUND COMES AROUND
A LESSON THAT WHAT WE LEARN
FOR SOME THINGS THAT WE GET IN LIFE
WE SOMETIMES DO NOT EARN

17. SOME PEOPLE.

SOME PEOPLE COME INTO OUR LIVES
AND CHANGE THE THINGS WE DO
THEY ALSO CHANGE THE WAY WE THINK
TO SEE THINGS DIFFERENT TOO
SOME PEOPLE SHOW US STRENGTH AND COURAGE
HOW TO DRY OUR TEARS
THE FRIENDSHIP MAY NOT GO BACK FAR
AND YET IT SEEMS LIKE YEARS
SOME PEOPLE WILL NOT BE FORGOT
THEIR LEGACY LIVES ON
I'M GLAD OUR PATHS HAD CHANCE TO CROSS
YOU WERE "A SPECIAL ONE"

WRITTEN IN MEMORY OF MY DEAR FRIEND
ANN JOYCE
WHO DIED 25TH JANUARY 2020

18. THE PEOPLE SHOW

WHAT A MERRY SIGHT
AND WHAT A MERRY SHOW
PEOPLE RUSHING HERE AND THERE
ALWAYS ON THE GO
THEY COME IN DIFFERENT SIZES
THEIR SHAPES ARE DIFFERENT TOO
MANY OF THEM DRESSED THE SAME
THE WAY MOST PEOPLE DO
ISN'T IT AMAZING
THE SIGHTS THAT WE CAN SEE
WHEN WE ARE PEOPLE WATCHING
WHEN OUR TIME IS FREE
MOST PEOPLE DO NOT REALISE
I'M WATCHING EVERY DAY
AND I WILL KEEP ON WATCHING
IN. MY OWN LITTLE WAY

19. TIME OF MEMORIES

IS TIME JUST A MEMORY
RUNNING THROUGH MY MIND?
AND WILL IT KEEP ON GOING
WHEN I LEAVE THIS WORLD BEHIND?
YOU CANNOT SEE OR HEAR IT
BUT YOU KNOW IT'S VERY REAL
YOU CANNOT EVEN TOUCH IT
BUT IT'S SOMETHING THAT YOU FEEL
YOU WAKE UP IN THE MORNING
WITH A MEMORY ON YOUR MIND
THEY KEEP ON COMING TO YOU
'TIL YOU LEAVE THE DAY BEHIND
EVEN IN THE NIGHTTIME
THE MEMORIES ARE REAL
IN YOUR DREAMS YOU HAVE AT NIGHT
IT'S SOMETHING YOU MIGHT FEEL
IS TIME JUST A MEMORY?
OR IS IT IN YOUR MIND?
DOES IT JUST KEEP GOING ON?
LEAVING US BEHIND?

20. IN A MODERN WORLD - 1

IN REAL LIFE TRUE FRIENDS ARE FRIENDS
NO MATTER WHAT YOU DO
IT DOESN'T MATTER WHERE YOU GO
THEY'LL STILL BE THERE FOR YOU
THE YEARS MAY PASS BEFORE YOU MEET
THEY STILL REMAIN A FRIEND
IT DOESN'T MATTER WHAT YOU SAY
THEY'LL BE THERE 'TIL THE END
BUT IN THE MODERN WORLD TODAY
OUR FRIENDS ARE NOW ONLINE
THEY ARE NOT REAL AND ARE NOT TRUE
BUT SAY THEY'RE FRIENDS OF MINE
WE NEVER MEET AND NEVER TALK
I WONDER IF THEY SEE
WHO I AM AND WHAT I AM?
THE PERSON WHICH IS ME
WILL THEY BE THERE IN YEARS TO COME?
WHEN YOU NEED A FRIEND
THEY ONLY WANT TO LIKE YOUR LIFE
AND PICTURES THAT YOU SEND

21. WEATHER THE CHANGE

HOW QUICKLY THE CHANGE
FROM DAY TO DAY
NO ONE QUITE KNOWS
WHAT'S COMING OUR WAY
ONE DAY IT'S SUNNY
THE NEXT DAY IT'S RAIN
THE CHANGE KEEPS ON HAPP'NIN'
AGAIN AND AGAIN
WILL THERE BE FOG?
OR WILL THERE BE SNOW?
WILL THERE BE GALES
TO MAKE THE FOG GO
THE WEATHERMAN SAYS
WHAT'S COMING THIS WAY
BUT THAT KEEPS ON CHANGING
EVERY DAY.

22. IN A MODERN WORLD – 2

HEAD IN THE CLOUDS
AND NOSE TO A PHONE
NO WONDER WE'RE OFTEN
FEELING ALONE
TAPPING A SCREEN
OR PHONE TO AN EAR
THERE'S THINGS YOU DON'T SEE
AND THINGS YOU DON'T HEAR
NO TIME TO WRITE
WITH PAPER AND PEN
JUST TAPPING AWAY
AGAIN AND AGAIN
HOW DO YOU SPELL
A SIMPLE SMALL WORD
JUST SHORTEN IT DOWN
BY HALF OR A THIRD
THE LETTER IS DYING
SLOWLY EACH DAY
TAP OUT YOUR MESSAGE
IT'S GONE ON ITS WAY
IT'S SAD BUT IT'S TRUE
BUT PEOPLE TODAY
HAVE LITTLE TO WRITE
AND SO MUCH TO SAY

23. BLACK AND WHITE

I SEE THE WORLD FOR WHAT IT IS
AND NOT IN BLACK AND WHITE
AND SOMETIMES WHEN I SEE SOME THINGS
THEY DO NOT SEEM QUITE RIGHT
TO SOME THE EDGES MAY BE BLURRED
I SEE THE COLOURS BRIGHT
I'LL SAY THINGS AS I SEE THEM
AND NOT SAY DAY IS NIGHT
SOME PEOPLE MAY BE SOMETIMES FOOLED
BY THINGS THAT AREN'T QUITE RIGHT
I WON'T BE TAKEN IN LIKE THEM
AND WON'T GIVE UP THE FIGHT
I WON'T BE FOOLED BY PEOPLE
THAT DO NOT FEEL QUITE RIGHT
NO MATTER WHAT THEY SAY OR DO
EITHER DAY OR NIGHT
I'VE LEARNED MY LESSONS SOME WERE HARD
AND NEARLY LOST THE FIGHT
BUT NOW I'M STRONG AND WISER
AND STANDING IN THE LIGHT.

24. LAST IN LINE

SLOWLY SLOWLY
ONE BY ONE
THE DAYS SLIPPED BY
THE YEARS WERE GONE.
WITHOUT CHILDREN
WITHOUT WIFE
THE OLD MAN LED
A LONELY LIFE.
JUST HIS MEMORIES
AS A FRIEND
WISHING THAT
HIS DAYS WOULD END.
WITHOUT FAMILY
NOW ALONE
THE LAST IN LINE
WOULD SOON BE GONE
NOT AFRAID
YET FEELING FEAR
KNOWING HE HAD
NO ONE NEAR.
WHERE TO GO
AND WHAT TO DO
THE LAST IN LINE
NEVER KNEW.
ALL ALONE
INTO THE NIGHT
FADING FAST
TO LOSE THE FIGHT.
NO ONE HEARD
AND NO ONE SAW
THE LAST MAN LAID
BEHIND HIS DOOR

25. BARGAIN HUNTERS

DON'T TRY JUST BUY
IS WHAT THEY DO
NO MATTER WHAT THE FIT
IT'S NOT THE LOOK
THEY'RE SEARCHING FOR
A BARGAIN'S WHAT THEY TOOK
THEY SEARCHED AROUND
UNTIL THEY FOUND
THE THINGS THAT THEY DON'T NEED
WITH JUST ONE GLANCE
THEY TOOK A CHANCE
AND ALSO TOOK THEIR CHOICE!

26. MOONLIGHT

AS MIDNIGHT CREEPS INTO THE WORLD
THE MOON IS SHINING BRIGHT
THE SHADOWS CAST A GHOSTLY MARK
FROM ITS LIGHT THAT NIGHT
NOTHING MOVED AND NOTHING STIRRED
AND PEACE REIGNED ALL AROUND
THE WORLD WAS SLEEPING PEACEFULLY
NOTHING MADE A SOUND
THE MINUTES TICKED THE HOURS ON
THE NIGHT TIME PASSING BY
AND SOON THE SUN WOULD RISE ABOVE
TO LIGHT THE DAYTIME SKY.

27. SINGING A SONG

HEY MR ROBIN
SITTING IN MY TREE
I'VE BEEN WATCHING YOU FOR AGES
IS IT ME YOU'VE COME TO SEE
YOUR BREAST IS VERY BRIGHT
AND YOUR SONG IS REALLY SWEET
TO LISTEN TO YOU EVERY DAY
REALLY IS A TREAT
YOU'RE JOINED BY MR BLACKBIRD
WHO SEEMS TO BE YOUR FRIEND
THE SONGS YOU SING TOGETHER
GIVES PLEASURE WITHOUT END
I LOVE THE SONGS YOU'RE SINGING
YOU SEEM TO HAVE NO FEAR
I'M GLAD YOU COME HERE EVERY DAY
TO GIVE MY HEART SOME CHEER

28. THE LONG GOODBYE

SOMETIMES I SIT HERE ALL ALONE AND WONDER
JUST WHERE IT IS THAT I KEEP GOING WRONG
THE PATH I'VE WALKED HAS NOT ALWAYS BEEN EASY
SOMETIMES IT FEELS LIKE IT HAS BEEN TOO LONG
I'VE BEEN TO VERY MANY DIFFERENT PLACES
AND SEEN SO MANY PEOPLE PASS BY ME
NO ONE SEEMS TO STAY AROUND FOR TOO LONG
AND ALL BECOME A FADING MEMORY

THE FLAMES THAT ONCE HAD FLICKERED NOW ARE EMBERS
THE LIGHT OUTSIDE IS SLOWLY DYING TOO
YOU CAN'T GET BACK THE PAST IT'S ALL NOW HISTORY
THERE'S REALLY NOTHING ANYONE CAN DO
TIME JUST SLIPS THROUGH HANDS LIKE RUNNING WATER
YOU CANNOT STOP IT PASSING ON ITS WAY
AND AS THE MOON AND SUN JUST GO ON SHINING
YOU KNOW THAT NIGHT WILL ALWAYS TURN TO DAY

THE PATH WE WALK HAS MANY HIDDEN DANGERS
THAT HIT US ALL JUST EVERY NOW AND THEN
WE RISE BACK UP - SHAKE OFF THE DUST
AND START OUR LIVES AGAIN
WE DON'T KNOW WHERE THE PATH WILL FINALLY TAKE US
WE REALLY ONLY KNOW ABOUT THE START
WE KNOW WE ONLY HAVE TO JUST KEEP GOING
AND EVERYONE HAS JUST TO PLAY THEIR PART

FOR SOME THE TIME TO SAY GOODBYE IS RIGHT NOW
AND THEN BECOME THAT FADING MEMORY
THE REST OF US WILL EVER TRAVEL ONWARDS
NOT KNOWING WHAT'S AHEAD OR WHAT WILL BE
YOU CANNOT CHANGE YOUR FATE OR CHANGE YOUR FUTURE
THESE THINGS ARE HIDDEN WELL AWAY FROM VIEW
YOU CANNOT CHANGE YOUR PAST IT TOO HAS HAPPENED
THERE'S REALLY NOTHING MUCH THAT YOU CAN DO.

29. A SIGN OF THE TIMES.

DID YOU EVER WATCH THE SUNSET
AS IT FELL ACROSS THE LAND?
DID YOU EVER SMELL THE BLOSSOM?
HOLD A FLOWER IN YOUR HAND?
DO YOU LISTEN TO THE BACKBIRD
AND HEAR THE SONGS HE SINGS?
YOU'VE TIME FOR ALL OF THIS NOW
AND MANY OTHER THINGS
THEY HAPPEN EVERY DAY
AND THEY'RE RIGHT IN FRONT OF YOU
THEY'VE BEEN GOING ON A LONG TIME
AND IT ISN'T SOMETHING NEW
WE HAVE TIME TO LOOK AND LISTEN
WE HAVE TIME NOW TO BEGIN
A TIME NOW TO APPRECIATE
THE WORLD WE'RE LIVING IN

30. NO REGRETS.

IF I COULD…
TURN BACK TIME I'D WALK AWAY
FROM SEVERAL THINGS THAT SPOIL MY DAY
I'D FIND THE THINGS THAT GAVE ME CHEER
THINGS THAT I ONCE HELD SO DEAR

IF I COULD…
THROW AWAY THE HURTFUL THINGS
THE PAIN AND SORROW THAT IT BRINGS
I'D FIND THE THINGS THAT MADE ME SMILE
HOLD ON TO THEM A LONG, LONG WHILE

IF I COULD…
GO BACK TO A YOUNGER DAY
I'D SAY THE THINGS I OUGHT TO SAY
DONE SOME THINGS I SHOULD HAVE DONE
ENJOYED MORE TIME OUT IN THE SUN.

IF I COULD…
PICK THE PIECES UP I'D DROPPED
KEPT ON WALKING AND NOT STOPPED
WOULD I BE WHERE I AM RIGHT NOW?
WOULD IT MATTER ANYHOW?

IF I COULD…
WOULD I REALLY IF I COULD?
SHOULD I REALLY IF I COULD?
IT'S TIME TO SAY "FORGIVE, FORGET"
AND LIVE MY LIFE WITH NO REGRET

31. CARE HOME BLUES

LADY IN THE WINDOW
LOOKING RATHER SAD
REMEMBERING HER HUSBAND
AND THE LIFE SHE HAD
THE YEARS HAVE RUSHED ON BY HER
SO NOW SHE SITS ALONE
HER FAMILY ALL BUSY
NOW THAT THEY HAVE GROWN
A GLASS OF JUICE BESIDE HER
THE TV TURNED UP HIGH
SHE DROPS HER BOOK ON TO THE FLOOR
AND GIVES A LITTLE SIGH
ALL SHE HAS TO DO ALL DAY
IS SIT THERE IN HER CHAIR
LOOKING OUT THE WINDOW
AND WISH SHE WASN'T THERE
REMEMBERING HER LIFE GONE BY
AND STROLLING THROUGH THE PARK
RETURNING BACK INTO THEIR HOME
BEFORE IT GOT TOO DARK
THE LADY IN THE CARE HOME
WILL SOON GO UP TO BED
THE SADNESS SHOWING IN HER EYES
SHE'LL REST HER WEARY HEAD

32. AND AFTER…

WE BORROWED THE EARTH
FOR SOMEWHERE TO LIVE
WE JUST KEEP ON TAKING
WITH NO TIME TO GIVE
WE JUST MAKE A MESS
BY THROWING AROUND
ALL OF OUR LITTER
DOWN ON THE GROUND
POLLUTING THE WATER
POLLUTING THE AIR
WITHOUT ANY THOUGHT
WITHOUT ANY CARE
WITH BULLET AND BOMB
WE'RE KILLING EACH OTHER
A SON AND A DAUGHTER
A FATHER A MOTHER
WITH DIRT AND POLLUTION
MOST OFTEN MAN MADE
WE'LL BLOCK OUT THE SUN
AND LEAVE US IN SHADE
WE'LL SMOTHER THE EARTH
THE WILDLIFE TOO
AND STOP MAN FROM BREATHING
IT'S WHAT WE WILL DO
IS IT TOO LATE
CAN MANKIND SURVIVE
WILL MOTHER NATURE
KEEP US ALIVE
CAN WE REPAIR
THE DAMAGE WE'VE DONE
OR WILL IT BE HERE
LONG AFTER WE'VE GONE?

33. DEAR FRIEND,

IT'S BEEN A LONG LONG TIME SINCE I LAST SAW YOU
THE DAYS PASS INTO WEEKS SO VERY FAST
BEFORE TOO LONG THE MONTHS HAVE COME BETWEEN US
AND SO ANOTHER YEAR HAS THEN GONE PAST
THE GARDEN LOOKS THE SAME IT DID LAST SUMMER
THE FLOWERS NOW ARE ALL OUT IN FULL BLOOM
THE BIRDS KEEP COMING BACK AGAIN FOR FEEDING
THEY ALWAYS SEEM TO CHASE AWAY THE GLOOM
I HAVEN'T EVEN PLANNED A LITTLE BREAK YET
I REALLY DO NOT KNOW JUST WHERE TO GO
PERHAPS I'LL STAY AT HOME AGAIN THIS SUMMER
AND HOPE THE SUMMER SUN WILL ONCE MORE SHOW
I MEANT TO CALL YOU ON THE PHONE LAST MONDAY
BUT TUESDAY CAME AROUND BEFORE I KNEW
AND SO I THOUGHT I'D WRITE TO YOU THIS LETTER
IT REALLY SEEMED THE ONLY THING TO DO
HOW ARE THINGS JUST NOW WHERE YOU ARE LIVING?
ARE YOU FIT AND ARE YOU KEEPING WELL?
DOES YOUR LANE LOOK LIKE IT ALWAYS HAS DONE?
AND HAVE YOU ANY NEWS THAT YOU CAN TELL?
I'LL TRY AND GET TO VISIT WHEN I CAN DO
I'LL STAY WITH YOU OR IN A B AND B
IT MAY BE FOR A WEEKEND OR A WHOLE WEEK
I THINK WE'LL SIMPLY HAVE TO WAIT AND SEE
YOU KNOW THE WIND THAT BLEW AGAIN LAST WINTER
BLEW THAT TREE DOWN RIGHT ACROSS THE ROAD
IT BLOCKED THE DRIVE AND BLOCKED THE GATE FOR TWO DAYS
WE HAD TO WAIT UNTIL THE COUNCIL SHOWED
WELL MY FRIEND THAT'S ALL THE NEWS I HAVE NOW
I'LL WAIT AGAIN UNTIL I HEAR FROM YOU
TAKE CARE STAY WELL I HOPE THAT YOU ARE HAPPY
AND SO I BID AGAIN A FOND ADIEU
YOURS IN FRIENDSHIP

COLIN

34. TOGETHER – FOREVER – AMEN

LIKE A PHOENIX I WILL RISE
BUT NOT BEFORE YOUR VERY EYES
MY SOUL WILL SOAR AND SLOWLY FLY ABOUT

SO DO NOT MOURN AND WEEP FOR ME
TIME HAS STOPPED AND I AM FREE
MY SOUL IS FULL OF LOVE THAT'S JUST FOR YOU

THIS PARTING NOW IS NOT GOODBYE
OUR FUTURE LIES BEYOND THE SKY
OUR SOULS WILL MEET ONCE MORE THEN FLY AWAY

TOGETHER ONCE AGAIN WE'LL BE
OUR TWO SOULS JOINED AS ONE.
TOGETHER ONCE AGAIN WE'LL BE
FOREVER AND AMEN

35. THE MAN HIMSELF

GENTLE GIANT TRUE AND KIND
MORE THAN JUST A FRIEND
GIVING OUT SUCH LOVE AND WARMTH
UNTIL THE VERY END
NO ONE WAS BELOW HIM
AND NO ONE WAS ABOVE
EVERYONE WAS EQUAL
HE SHOWED THAT IN HIS LOVE
SUPPORTIVE AND SO CARING
THROUGHOUT THE DAYS AND YEARS
READY JUST TO SHARE WITH YOU
YOUR LAUGHTER AND YOUR TEARS
HE WILL NOT BE FORGOTTEN
HIS MEM'RY CARRIES ON
HIS SPIRIT IS AROUND US
ALTHOUGH HE HAS NOW GONE.

36. IS THAT ALL WE DO..?

I SIT, I WATCH, I WONDER
WHAT IT'S ALL ABOUT
THE LONGER THAT I STAY HERE
MAKES ME WANT TO SHOUT
WILL ANYBODY NOTICE?
CAN ANYBODY HEAR?
WHAT I TRY TO TELL ABOUT
IS DRAWING VERY NEAR
I FEAR ABOUT THE DANGER
AND WHAT WILL HAPPEN NOW
IS IT REALLY TOO LATE?
TO STOP IT ANYHOW
THE FUTURE CAN BE DANGEROUS
OUR PAST IS DEAD AND GONE
CAN WE LEARN OUR LESSON?
AS THE PRESENT PASSES ON
DOES IT REALLY MATTER?
DO WE REALLY CARE?
AS IT FAST APPROACHES
WE STAND, WE WAIT, WE STARE.

37. THE END…

YOU KNOW THERE'S NO POINT RUNNING
AND YOU KNOW YOU CANNOT HIDE
IF THE DEVIL DOES NOT GET YOU
LET AN ANGEL BE YOUR GUIDE
YOU DON'T KNOW WHEN IT'S COMING
BUT YOU'LL KNOW WHEN IT IS HERE
IT CREEPS UP FROM BEHIND YOU
AND YOU HAVE NO TIME TO FEAR
IT MAY NOT COME TOMORROW
IF IT DID NOT COME TODAY
BUT ONE DAY WHEN YOU LEAST EXPECT
IT GETS RIGHT IN YOUR WAY
FORGET THOSE SENSELESS WORRIES
THEY'LL ONLY GET YOU DOWN
LIVE YOUR LIFE AND WEAR A SMILE
THROW AWAY YOUR FROWN
YOU'VE NO TIME FOR REGRETTING
JUST GET OUT THERE AND LIVE
MAKE THE MOST OF ALL YOU CAN
FORGET AND PLEASE FORGIVE
YOU'LL NEVER GET BACK TIME YOU'VE LOST
FOR WHEN IT'S GONE IT'S GONE
THE END MAY COME AT ANY TIME
AND WHEN IT'S DONE IT'S DONE

38. SILENCE IS GOLDEN

THE SILENCE OF A WOODLAND
IS BROKEN BY THE SOUND
OF BRANCHES MOVING IN A BREEZE
HIGH ABOVE THE GROUND
AS PEACE DESCENDS ACROSS THE LAND
THERE'S LITTLE TO BE HEARD
A RUSTLE IN THE UNDERGROWTH
THE TWITTER OF A BIRD
THE SILENCE ONLY BROKEN
EVERY NOW AND THEN
UNTIL THE DARK OF NIGHTIME ENDS
AND DAYTIME STARTS AGAIN

39. ME, ME, ME?

WHY DON'T WE CARE ABOUT ONE ANOTHER?
AND WHY ALL THIS SELFISH GREED?
IT SEEMS IT'S ONLY ME, ME, ME
NOT CARING WHAT OTHERS MIGHT NEED
IT'S TIME TO STOP AND TIME TO THINK
AND SHOW WE REALLY CARE
LET THOSE PEOPLE LESS WELL OFF
KNOW THAT WE ARE THERE
THERE TO HELP IN TIME OF NEED
THERE TO SHARE OUR LOVE
SHOW IT'S NOT JUST ME, ME, ME
AND STOP THIS PUSH AND SHOVE
WE'RE IN THIS WORLD TOGETHER
LET'S PROVE THAT THIS IS TRUE
SHOW SOME THOUGHT AND KINDNESS
FOR THOSE WHO MIGHT NEED YOU
ONE DAY YOU MIGHT NEED OTHERS
AND THEN ONE DAY YOU'LL SEE
JUST HOW MEAN AND THOUGHTLESS
IS THIS ME, ME, ME, ME, ME.

40. THROUGH IT ALL…

I STILL SEE THE SUN THROUGH MY WINDOW
AND STILL HEAR THE BIRDS IN THE TREES
I STILL SEE THE FLOWERS NOW BLOOMING
AND STILL FEEL THE COOL OF A BREEZE
I STILL WALK A LANE IN THE SUNSHINE
AND STILL SEE THE GRASS THAT IS GREEN
I STILL SEE THE VALLEYS AND HILLSIDES
AND STILL SEE A BEAUTIFUL SCENE
I STILL HEAR THE BABBLING WATERS
AND STILL SEE THE MOON SHINE AT NIGHT
I STILL FEEL THE WARMTH OF THE SUNSHINE
AND STILL SEE A WONDERFUL SIGHT
I STILL SEE THE WORLD IN ITS GLORY
AND STILL FEEL I WANT TO BE PART
I STILL SEE THE WONDER IN NATURE
THROUGH IT ALL I FEEL JOY IN MY HEART

41. REALITY CHECK

GREEN GROWS THE GRASS
UPON THE OTHER SIDE
UNTIL YOU CROSS ON OVER
AND FIND SOMEBODY LIED
SO WELCOME TO MY PARLOUR
SAID THE SPIDER TO THE FLY
WHY IS IT THAT YOU LOOK SO SAD?
WHY IS IT THAT YOU CRY?
YOUR GLASSES LOOK SO PRETTY
A LOVELY SHADE OF RED
DON'T YOU LIKE THE THINGS YOU SEE
OR LIKE THE THINGS I SAID?
THE BRIDGE YOU CROSSED IS BURNING
THE WATERS FLOWING DEEP
YOUR EYES ARE FEELING TIRED
AND YET YOU CANNOT SLEEP
NOT EVERYTHING IS WHAT YOU THINK
AND EVEN QUITE AS GOOD
AS YOU SIT UPON YOUR FENCE
MADE OF BROKEN WOOD
SO STAY SAT ON YOUR WOODEN FENCE
AND DO NOT HEAVE A SIGH
TOMORROW IS ANOTHER DAY
TO WATCH THE WORLD GO BY

42. THROUGH STORMS OF TROUBLED TIMES

I SPENT SOME TIME IN WIND AND RAIN
WHEN CLOUDS GOT IN THE WAY
LOOKING OUT FOR SUNSHINE
EACH AND EVERY DAY
AND STORMS THAT PASSED BY OVERHEAD
OFTEN MADE ME SHAKE
WITH COLD THAT SEEMED TO PENETRATE
WITH EVERY BREATH I'D TAKE
I TRIED TO DODGE THE RAINDROPS
FALLING FROM THE SKY
BUT STILL THEY SOAKED ME TO THE SKIN
THEY NEVER PASSED ME BY
THE CLOUDS ABOVE WERE DARK AND GREY
NOT OFTEN FLUFFY WHITE
I WISHED THAT THEY WOULD DISAPPEAR
AND STAY OUT OF MY SIGHT
THE DAYS THAT I FELT SUNSHINE
ON MY BACK SO WARM
ALSO WARMED MY HEART AND SOUL
AND MADE ME FEEL QUITE CALM
ONCE THE STORMS HAVE PASSED ON BY
I START TO FEEL MORE STRONG
NO LONGER FEEL THE FEAR I HAD
WHEN DARK CLOUDS CAME ALONG
AND WITH EACH DAY THAT PASSES BY
I'LL WALK ANOTHER MILE
WITH HEAD HELD HIGH AND SHOULDERS BACK
AND WITH A CHEERY SMILE.

43. HAPPY!

SING A SONG OF SIXPENCE
A POCKETFUL OF RYE
I CAN SEE A BLACKBIRD
HIGH UP IN THE SKY
HE IS FAT AND BLACK AND ROUND
AND SOON SITTING IN MY TREE
AND I'M FEELING PRETTY CERTAIN
THAT HE SINGS HIS SONG FOR ME
HE JUMPS DOWN IN THE BIRD BATH
AND SPLASHES ALL AROUND
WITH WATER GOING EVERYWHERE
HE MAKES A JOYFUL SOUND
THEN HOPPING ON THE TABLE
HE HAS HIMSELF A MEAL
HOW HAPPY CAN THIS SIMPLE BIRD
REALLY MAKE ME FEEL?

44. A LESSON IN LIFE

WHEN I WAS SMALL AND TREES SEEMED TALL
WE'D CLIMB THEM IF WE COULD
SITTING IN THE BRANCHES
AND FEELING PRETTY GOOD
LOOKING ROUND ON TO THE GROUND
SO MANY FEET BELOW
WE DIDN'T EVEN FEEL A CHILL
WHEN A BREEZE WOULD BLOW
THE RUSTLING LEAVES UP IN THE TREES
SOUNDED VERY SWEET
AND SO WE'D HOLD ON CAREFULLY
USING HANDS AND FEET
WE DIDN'T SLIP OR LOSE OUR GRIP
AS WE CLIMBED THOSE TREES
WE NEVER REALLY HURT OURSELVES
JUST SOMETIMES GRAZED OUR KNEES
OH WHAT A JOY FOR GIRL OR BOY
SUCH A TREE COULD GIVE
WHILE LEARNING HOW TO GET ALONG
AND LEARNING HOW TO LIVE

45. RUNNING AWAY?

LOOKING OVER MY SHOULDER
AT THINGS I MIGHT SEE
AND RUNNING AWAY
FROM THINGS THAT MIGHT BE
A MEMORY FADING
BUT STILL IN MY VIEW
TELLING ME THINGS
I WISH WERE NOT TRUE
THINGS THAT REMIND ME
OF DAYS IN MY PAST
AND PEOPLE I KNEW
ALL GONE TOO FAST
YOU CAN'T RUN AWAY
YOU CAN'T EVEN HIDE
THE MEM'RIES ARE LOCKED
DEEP DOWN INSIDE

46. TEDDY BEAR LOVE

COME HERE BESIDE ME
FOR JUST A SHORT WHILE
WITH WARMTH FROM YOUR HUG
I'LL ONCE AGAIN SMILE
THE COMFORT YOU BRING ME
ON MANY LONG NIGHT
IS STILL ALWAYS WITH ME
AT BREAKING OF LIGHT
WE'VE KNOWN ONE ANOTHER
FOR MANY LONG YEARS
SHARED MANY SMILES WITH YOU
SHARED MANY TEARS
YOU DON'T TURN YOUR BACK
AND YOU DON'T TURN AWAY
YOU'LL ALWAYS BE NEAR ME
EVERY DAY
HOW DO I SHOW THANKS
FOR ALL THAT WE SHARE
MY LOYAL AND LOVING
DEAR TEDDY BEAR

47. IMMORTALITY?

THEIR NAMES ARE ALL CARVED OUT IN STONE
SOME FOR MANY YEARS
THEY ALL TOLD DIFFERENT STORIES
WITH LAUGHTER AND WITH TEARS
A LOT ARE LONG FORGOTTEN NOW
SWALLOWED BY THE PAST
WITH MANY NEW ONES JOINING ON
NO ONE WILL BE LAST
TIMES WILL CHANGE AS YEARS GO BY
BUT ONE THING STAYS THE SAME
AND HOW WE CLOSE THE FINAL PAGE
MAY HAVE A DIFFERENT NAME
BUT STILL THE NAMES ARE CARVED IN STONE
FOR ANYONE TO SEE
A NAME, A DATE, SOMETIMES AND AGE
OUR IMMORTALITY

48. WAITING…?

IN THE DARK OF NIGHT-TIME HOURS
WHEN EVERYONE'S ASLEEP
SOMEWHERE IN THE MOONLIGHT SHADOWS
WHERE YOUR THOUGHTS WILL CREEP
STOLEN MOMENTS IN THE NIGHT
MEMORIES OF SOME DREAMS
IN THE MIDNIGHT DARKNESS
NOTHING'S WHAT IT SEEMS
SILENCE BROKEN BY A CRY
IN THE EARLY HOURS
A RUSTLE IN THE TREE TOP LEAVES
OR DOWN AMONG THE FLOWERS
HALF REMEMBERED DREAMS YOU HAD
OTHERS YOU FORGET
THEN WOKEN FROM A NIGHTMARE
IN A VERY DAMP COLD SWEAT
AND LYING IN THE DARKNESS
AWAITING FOR THE DAWN
TO CHASE AWAY THE SHADOWS
AT THE BREAK OF MORN'

49. HISTORY LESSON

IF HISTORY'S TOLD IN PHOTOGRAPHS
I WONDER WHAT'S THE TALE
ALL OF THEM IN BLACK AND WHITE
SOME OF THEM QUITE PALE
PEOPLE WHO DO NOT HAVE NAMES
AND PLACES I DON'T KNOW
SOME PICTURES BENT ON CORNERS
WITH CREASES THAT JUST GROW
THERE'S NO ONE LEFT THAT I CAN ASK
AND SOON THERE'LL BE JUST ME
THOSE FACES NOW FORGOTTEN
BECOMING HISTORY
WILL ANYBODY WONDER?
WILL ANYBODY CARE?
WHEN I AM PART OF HISTORY
TO EVERYONE OUT THERE

50. WOULD I…?

IF I KNEW THEN
WHAT I KNOW NOW
WOULD IT CHANGE THINGS ANYHOW?
WITH TIME TO LOOK
BEFORE I LEAP
WOULD I COUNT YEARS OR JUST COUNT SHEEP?

IF BLACK WERE WHITE
AND DAY WAS NIGHT
WOULD ALL MY THOUGHTS HAVE WINGS?
IF I LIVED DREAMS
AND PLANNED MY SCHEMES
WOULD I HAVE LOVELY THINGS?

IF I TOOK TIME
AND I STOOD STILL
WOULD LIFE STAND STILL FOR ME?
WITH EYES SHUT TIGHT
WHEN LOOKING BACK
WOULD I LIKE WHAT I SEE?

51. DOGGIE LOVE

BERTIE'S LIKE A GREAT BIG BEAR
THE KIND WE ALL CALL "TED"
YOU WANT TO HUG AND CUDDLE HIM
AND TAKE HIM TO YOUR BED
HE'S BIG AND SOFT AND BEAUTIFUL
AND REALLY LOVES ME SO
HE ALWAYS GETS A LOT OF FUSS
WHEREVER WE MAY GO
HIS TAIL IS WAGGING CONSTANTLY
HE BOUNDS AROUND A LOT
HE'S ALWAYS FULL OF ENERGY
A LOT MORE THAN I'VE GOT
HIS EYES ARE BRIGHT AND SPARKLING
I'M SURE IF HE COULD TALK
HE'D ASK ME FOR HIS BISCUITS
OR ASK ME FOR A WALK
MY BERTIE IS A RASCAL
I REALLY LOVE HIM SO
HE ALWAYS LIFTS MY SPIRITS
WHENEVER I FEEL LOW

52. FAILING MEMORY – 1.

ARE DAYS REALLY DIFFERENT NOW
TO HOW THEY USED TO BE
AS I REMEMBER SUMMER DAYS
WE SEEMED TO BE CAREFREE
THE DAYS FELT VERY HOT AND LONG
WE PLAYED DOWN ON THE BEACH
SKIMMING STONES AND JUMPING WAVES
WITH NOTHING OUT OF REACH
THE WINTER DAYS WERE CHILLY THEN
WITH SNOW DOWN ON THE GROUND
AND EVERY DAY WAS DIFFERENT
AS WE PLAYED AROUND
SLEDGING DOWN THE HILLSIDE
SLIDING ON THE ICE
THEN SITTING BY THE FIRESIDE
COZY WARM AND NICE
DOES MY MEMORY FAIL ME
ARE THINGS SO DIFFERENT NOW
AS I'M GROWING OLDER
THEY'RE CHANGING ANYHOW

53. PASSING BY

I JUMPED IN THE CAR
TO GO FOR A DRIVE
TO SEE IF THE WORLD
WAS REALLY ALIVE
OUT IN THE COUNTRY
DRIVE DOWN A LANE
TO PLACES I'VE BEEN
AGAIN AND AGAIN
EVERYWHERE QUIET
AND EVERYWHERE STILL
DOWN IN A DALE
ON TOP OF A HILL
LEAVES ON THE GROUND
THEY'D STARTED TO FALL
I HARDLY BELIEVED
MY EYES AT ALL
NO SUN IN THE SKY
JUST CLOUD EVERYWHERE
FIELDS LOOKING EMPTY
BARREN AND BARE
SILENT AND STILL
WITH NO ONE IN SIGHT
THE SKY LOOKING EMPTY
NO BIRDS WERE IN FLIGHT
AUTUMN WAS COMING
SUMMER WAS PAST
MY EYES MISTED OVER
SO VERY FAST
WHERE HAD IT GONE
THE TIME THAT WE HAD
PASSED BY SO QUICKLY
AND MADE ME FEEL SAD

54. COVID 19 2020

WE'RE HAVING TO BE DIFFERENT
SO WE DO THE BEST WE CAN
WE KEEP OUR SOCIAL DISTANCE
FROM OUR FELLOW MAN
WE COVER HALF OUR FACES
AND NOBODY CAN SEE
THE PAIN AND ALL THE ANGUISH
THAT'S INSIDE YOU AND ME
LIFE IS VERY DIFFERENT
AND CHANGED SO VERY FAST
AND NO ONE REALLY SEEMS TO KNOW
HOW LONG IT WILL LAST
PERHAPS IT'S TIME TO STOP AND THINK
ABOUT YOUR FELLOW MAN
SHOW MORE LOVE AND CARING
ANY WAY YOU CAN
WE DO NOT NEED TO RUSH AROUND
STRIVE AT GREED AND GAIN
AND THIS SHOULD BE A LESSON
TO PUT AN END TO PAIN
THE PAIN OF MODERN LIVING
WHERE MANY DO NOT CARE
WE'RE ALL IN THIS TOGETHER
NO MATTER WHO OR WHERE.

55. THE GAME

ISN'T IT AMAZING
WHEN YOU LOOK AROUND
AT ALL THE SHAPES AND SIZES
THAT THERE CAN BE FOUND
I SEE THEM WALKING BY ME
OR WATCH THEM DRIVING BY
WHEN I'M PEOPLE WATCHING
ALL JUST CATCH MY EYE
THERE ARE BIG ONES THERE ARE SMALL ONES
THEY COME IN THIN OR ROUND
SOME ARE TALKING QUITE A LOT
SOME DON'T MAKE A SOUND
EVERYONE IS DIFFERENT
NO TWO ARE THE SAME
EVERYONE I'M SEEING
IN THIS PEOPLE WATCHING GAME

56. THE ROSE

THE LAST ROSE OF SUMMER IS BLOOMING
JUST BEFORE WINTER SETS IN
WHILE LEAVES ARE FALLING AROUND IT
BEFORE THE SNOWFLAKES BEGIN.

THE LAST ROSE THAT'S LEFT ALONE BLOOMING
REMINDS US THAT SUMMER'S NOW GONE
TELLS US THE YEAR'S ALMOST OVER
WINTER WILL SOON COME ALONG.

THE LAST ROSE OF SUMMER IS PRETTY
AND STILL SMELLS AS SWEET AS THE FIRST
IT'S PETALS STILL HAVE A COLOUR
MAKES MY HEART FEEL FIT TO BURST

57. SOLITARY

DO YOU EVER FEEL ALONE
LIKE NO ONE ELSE IS THERE?
DO YOU WONDER TO YOURSELF
DOES ANYBODY CARE?
WHEN ALL AROUND IS CHANGING
AND NOTHING STAYS THE SAME
DAY BY DAY AND WEEK BY WEEK
IT REALLY IS A SHAME.
NO ONE SEEMS TO NOTICE
DOES ANYBODY SEE?
STANDING THERE BY ITSELF
A LONE AND SINGLE TREE.

58. PRESENT DAY LIVING

MY HEART IS CRYING OUT WITH PAIN
WHEN IT SEES THIS HATE
CAN'T WE STOP WHAT'S HAPPENING
BEFORE IT IS TOO LATE
WE'RE KILLING ONE ANOTHER
WITHOUT A REASON WHY
IT ISN'T OURS TO DECIDE
WHEN SOMEONE ELSE SHOULD DIE
WE'RE SLOWLY LOSING ALL RESPECT
AND DO NOT SEEM TO CARE
WHAT DESTRUCTION WE MIGHT CAUSE
IT'S 'ROUND US EVERYWHERE
SOME PEOPLE DO NOT REALISE
THE HURTING THAT THEY BRING
WITH THE ACTS OF VIOLENCE
ON ALL AND EVERYTHING
IT'S TIME TO STOP AND MAKE AMENDS
FOR ALL THAT WE HAVE DONE
IT'S TIME TO TURN THE WORLD AROUND
BEFORE OUR CHANCE HAS GONE

59. SOMETHING STRANGE

ISN'T IT FUNNY, ISN'T IT STRANGE
AND ISN'T IT RATHER QUEER
ANOTHER DAY, ANOTHER WEEK
AND THEN ANOTHER YEAR
I CAN'T UNDERSTAND HOW TIME PASSES BY
SO VERY FAST FOR ME
AND YET SEEMS TO GO SO VERY SLOW
FOR EVERYONE ELSE THAT I SEE
EVERYONE SAYS THAT TIME PASSES BY
FASTER THE OLDER YOU GET
BUT LOOKING AT PEOPLE OLDER THAN ME
THERE'S SOMETHING I JUST DON'T GET
I'M AGEING AS FAST AS EVERYONE ELSE
BUT OTHERS HAVE NO CHANGE
THEY JUST LOOK THE SAME AS THEY ALWAYS HAVE
WHICH REALLY SEEMS QUITE STRANGE.

60. UNCERTAIN OF THE CERTAIN

I DON'T KNOW WHERE I'M GOING
BUT I KNOW WHERE I HAVE BEEN
I DON'T KNOW WHAT I'LL FIND THERE
BUT I KNOW WHAT I HAVE SEEN
I DON'T KNOW WHAT I'LL SEE THERE
BUT I KNOW WHAT I HAVE HEARD
I DON'T KNOW WHO WILL BE THERE
BUT I KNOW WITH WHOM I'VE SHARED
I DON'T KNOW WHAT WILL HAPPEN
BUT KNOW WHAT I HAVE DONE
I DON'T KNOW WHERE THE JOURNEY ENDS
BUT KNOW WHERE IT BEGUN
I DON'T KNOW WHEN THE TIME WILL BE
BUT KNOW I'M IN THE NOW
I DON'T KNOW HOW IT HAPPENS
BUT KNOW IT WILL SOMEHOW
I DON'T KNOW IF I'M FRIGHTENED
BUT KNOW THAT I'M NOT SCARED
I DON'T KNOW WILL I BE ALONE?
BUT KNOW THE LOVE I'VE SHARED

61. DOGGIE LOVE - 2

I HAVE A DOG TO LOVE ME
AND I HAVE A DOG TO LOVE
I WONDER WHERE HE CAME FROM
COULD IT BE FROM GOD ABOVE
HE GIVES HIS LOVE WITHOUT STRINGS
AND YET HE BINDS MY HEART
EVERY DAY AND EVERY NIGHT
HE'S DONE THIS FROM THE START
HE FILLS MY LIFE WITH LOVE AND JOY
AND ASKS FOR LITTLE BACK
HE FILLS MY LIFE WITH COLOUR
NOT JUST WHITE AND BLACK
I KNOW THAT HE'D PROTECT ME
IF DANGER LAY AHEAD
HE UNDERSTANDS MY EVERY MOVE
AND EVERYTHING I'VE SAID
WE HAVE AN UNDERSTANDING
A SIMPLE LITTLE PACT
ONE WE MADE SO LONG AGO
AND STILL REMAINS A FACT
I'LL LOVE HIM AND TAKE CARE OF HIM
HOWEVER LONG THAT TAKES
HE PUT HIS TRUST AND FAITH IN ME
MY RIGHTS AND MY MISTAKES
HIS LOVE HAS NO CONDITIONS
HIS LOVE IS PURE AND STRONG
I'LL GIVE HIM LOVE BACK IN RETURN
THROUGHOUT HIS WHOLE LIFE LONG

62. TREES

I REMEMBER SUMMER DAYS
AND PLAYING IN THE TREES
FALLING DOWN AND GETTING UP
WE'D ONLY GRAZE OUR KNEES
AND EVEN ON THOSE SUMMER DAYS
THAT SOMETIMES TURNED OUT WET
WE'D STILL BE OUT THERE PLAYING
NO CARE HOW WET WE'D GET
BUILDING SWINGS AND MAKING SLIDES
WHAT ELSE COULD THERE BE
BUT ALL THE FUN AND FREEDOM
FROM JUST A SINGLE TREE
WHAT MORE FUN COULD WE HAVE
IN A SINGLE DAY
THAN BEING IN A WOODLAND
WITH LOTS OF GAMES TO PLAY
WE KNEW THOSE TREES BY SHAPE OR NAME
THEY REALLY WERE A FRIEND
WHY DID THOSE DAYS OF SUMMER FUN
EVER HAVE TO END
AND NOW THOSE TREES ARE ALL ALONE
AND NO ONE GOES TO PLAY
THEY'RE STILL THERE STANDING STRONG AND TALL
TO THIS VERY DAY

63. STONES

THERE WAS A GREAT BIG PILE OF STONE
I WOULD NOT CALL IT RUBBLE
WE WENT AND PLAYED THERE MANY HOURS
WITHOUT ANY TROUBLE
IMAGINATIONS RUNNING WILD
WE REALLY HAD GREAT FUN
PLAYING OUT THERE WHEN WE COULD
IN THE SUMMER SUN
SOMEDAYS IT WAS A SPACESHIP
WAY OUT IN OUTER SPACE
ANOTHER DAY AN ISLAND
OR SOME FORGOTTEN PLACE
OUR FUN IT HAD NO BOUNDARIES
IT JUST WENT ON AND ON
WE DID WHAT WE DECIDED
UNTIL THE DAY WAS DONE

64. WATER

WHO BOTHERED IF WE ALL GOT WET
NO MATTER HOW OR WHERE
IN THE RAIN OR FLOWING STREAM
WE DID NOT REALLY CARE
AS LONG AS WE HAD LOTS OF FUN
SPLASHING ALL AROUND
IN THE STREAM OR IN A PUDDLE
THAT'S WHERE WE'D BE FOUND
FEEDING DUCKS DOWN AT THE POND
OR BEING BY THE SEA
AS LONG AS THERE WAS WATER
THAT'S WHERE WE LIKED TO BE
SOMETIMES WE WORE OUR WELLIES
SOMETIMES IT WAS BARE FEET
YOU OR I OR OTHER KIDS
WHO LIVED JUST DOWN THE STREET
WHAT WAS THIS DRAW TO WATER
I NEVER REALLY KNEW
WE ALWAYS KNEW THAT WE WOULD FIND
LOTS OF THINGS TO DO

65. DEJA – VU ?

SHOULD HISTORY REPEAT ITSELF
QUITE AS FAST AS THIS?
OR IS THERE SOMETHING HAPPENING
AND REALLY NOW AMISS?
IT DOES NOT SEEM THAT LONG AGO
WE WERE IN THIS PLACE
AND HERE WE ARE NOW ONCE AGAIN
WE KNOW WHAT WE NOW FACE
IT'S LIKE WE'RE ON A CAROUSEL
FOREVER GOING ROUND
NO STARTING AND NO ENDING
TO WHERE OUR JOURNEY'S BOUND
WE'VE SEEN IT ALL NOT LONG AGO
WE LIVE IT ALL ONCE MORE
AND VERY LITTLE SEEMS TO CHANGE
IT'S ALL JUST LIKE BEFORE
IS THIS SOMETHING FROM MY DREAMS
OR IS IT DEJA-VU?
IS HISTORY REPEATING?
AND DO YOU FEEL IT TOO?

66. COUNTING

WHEN I COUNT MY BLESSINGS
I COUNT THEM ONE BY ONE
AND VERY SOON WHEN COUNTING
I FIND MY FINGERS GONE
I CARRY ON WITH CHECKING
AND COUNTING ON MY TOES
AND VERY SOON THE NUMBER
I HAVE JUST SIMPLY GROWS
AND WHEN I TAKE A LOOK OUTSIDE
IT'S WHEN I REALISE
THERE'S OTHER MANY BLESSINGS
RIGHT BEFORE MY EYES
THERE IS NO POINT IN COUNTING
THE NUMBER IS TOO GREAT
I'LL JUST ACCEPT THE BLESSINGS
BEFORE IT IS TOO LATE

67. ONLY THE LONELY

A SINGLE TEAR ROLLS DOWN HER CHEEK
EVERY NIGHT OF EVERY WEEK
ALL ALONE SAT IN HER CHAIR
NO ONE KNOWS THAT SHE IS THERE
NO ONE LEFT TO HOLD HER TIGHT
KISS OR HUG HER LATE AT NIGHT

A SINGLE TEAR SITS ON HIS FACE
LOOKING VERY OUT OF PLACE
SITTING LONELY IN HIS CHAIR
NO ONE KNOWS THAT HE IS THERE
NO ONE THERE TO KEEP HIM WARM
OR KEEP HIM SAFE AWAY FROM HARM

LOTS OF TEARS LOOK OUT OF PLACE
LEAVING STREAKS UPON A FACE
ALL ALONE AND NO ONE THERE
WITHOUT A THOUGHT WITHOUT A CARE
NO ONE LEFT TO SHARE A LIFE
THE COLD JUST CUTTING LIKE A KNIFE

SO MANY TEARS UPON A FACE
IT REALLY IS A SAD DISGRACE
TOO MANY PEOPLE ON THEIR OWN
DOES NO ONE CARE THEY'RE ALL ALONE
NO ONE STOPS WHEN PASSING BY
THAT'S WHY LONELY PEOPLE CRY

68. JUST A DREAMER?

YESTERDAY'S DREAMS FOR TOMORROW
WILL THEY EVER COME TRUE?
OR WILL THEY JUST FADE IN THE DAYTIME?
LIKE SO MANY DREAMS OFTEN DO
WHEN I AWAKE AND REMEMBER
THE DREAMS THAT I HAD IN THE NIGHT
I TRY AND HOLD ON TO THE MEMORY
AS IT FADES IN THE FIRST MORNING LIGHT
AND WHEN I DREAM OF TOMORROW
IT ALWAYS SEEMS REAL AND SO TRUE
THAT WHEN I AWAKE IN THE MORNING
I FEEL LIKE I'VE LIVED THE DREAM THROUGH
REALITY HITS BACK SO QUICKLY
I KNOW IT WAS JUST IN MY SLEEP
THE DREAM FOR TODAY OR TOMORROW
WAS A DREAM I ALWAYS WILL KEEP

69. MOVING ON…

I CAN'T SEE WHERE I'VE BEEN
AND CANT'T SEE WHERE I'M GOING
I JUST KEEP STUMBLING FORWARD
WITHOUT REALLY KNOWING
NOTHING SEEMS TO BE QUITE CLEAR
I SLOWLY MOVE ALONG
UNCERTAIN OF MY WAY AHEAD
IN CASE I MIGHT GO WRONG
IT SEEMS TO TAKE FOREVER
TO GET FROM A TO B
BECAUSE OF ALL THIS THICK FOG
I REALLY CANNOT SEE

70. IN MEMORIAM

THE MEMORIES STILL LINGER
THE PAIN STAYS IN MY HEART
AT TIMES I FIND IT VERY HARD
TO THINK WE HAD TO PART
THE YEARS WE SPENT TOGETHER
AND ALL WE USED TO DO
STILL SO FRESH WITHIN MY MIND
AS IF IT ALL WAS NEW
AND TIME HAS PASSED SO QUICKLY
IT DOESN'T SEEM QUITE REAL
I TELL MYSELF IT'S OVER
IT'S JUST NOT HOW I FEEL
I FEEL YOUR SPIRIT NEAR ME
I FEEL YOUR GUIDING HAND
I KNOW THAT YOU ARE WATCHING ME
ALL ACROSS THE LAND
I NEVER WILL FORGET YOU
THE MEMORIES WILL STAY
I KNOW I'LL ALWAYS LOVE YOU
FOREVER AND A DAY

71. REALLY THERE?

FROM OUT THE CORNER OF MY EYE
HIDDEN FROM MY MIND
THERE'S SOMETHING THERE THAT I CAN SEE
BUT CANNOT SEEM TO FIND
I TURN MY HEAD TO TAKE A LOOK
BUT SOMEHOW IT'S NOT THERE
I CANNOT SEEM TO SEE IT
IF I SIT AND STARE
I START TO WONDER IF IT'S REAL
IF IT'S THERE AT ALL
IT SOMETIMES SEEMS TO BE QUITE BIG
AND SOMETIMES VERY SMALL
I TURN MY HEAD QUITE QUICKLY
TO TRY AND CATCH IT OUT
IT MOVES MUCH QUICKER THAN I CAN
WHICH CAUSES ME TO DOUBT
I KNOW I AM NOT SEEING THINGS
I'VE SEEN THEM ALL BEFORE
IT'S JUST THAT WHEN I TRY TO LOOK
I FIND IT'S THERE NO MORE

72. THE JOURNEY

WHEN I WAS JUST A LITTLE BOY
THE YEARS THAT LAY AHEAD
WERE SOMETHING IN THE FUTURE
OR SOMETHING SOMEONE SAID
THE DAYS WERE MEANT FOR PLAYING
FOR LEARNING AND TO GROW
GAINING ALL OUR KNOWLEDGE
FROM PEOPLE IN THE KNOW
WHEN I WAS JUST A LITTLE BOY
OUR WOES AND CARES WERE SMALL
WE DIDN'T WORRY VERY MUCH
WE THOUGHT WE HAD IT ALL

WHEN I WAS JUST A GROWING YOUTH
MY CHILDHOOD YEARS WERE PAST
I STILL HAD MUCH I HAD TO LEARN
AND DO IT VERY FAST
THE FUTURE KEPT ON COMING
AND I KEPT MOVING ON
TIME TO MOVE IN TO THE WORLD
MY SCHOOL DAYS NOW WERE GONE
WHEN I WAS JUST A GROWING YOUTH
MY WORLD BEGAN TO GROW
THINGS WERE CHANGING ALL THE TIME
THINGS I LEARNT TO KNOW

WHEN I WAS JUST A YOUNG MAN
WITH CHOICES TO BE MADE
MOVING FROM THE FAMILY HOME
FUTURE PLANS WERE LAID
WORK WAS A CAREER NOW
WE HAD TO SETTLE DOWN
HOME WAS NOW A HOUSE
ON THE OUTSKIRTS OF A TOWN
WHEN I WAS JUST A YOUNG MAN
THINGS WERE NOT THE SAME
WE HAD TO TAKE LIFE SERIOUSLY
NO LONGER WAS A GAME

THE JOURNEY – (CONT)

WHEN I WAS AN OLDER MAN
IN MY MIDDLE YEARS
PEOPLE CAME AND PEOPLE WENT
I STARTED TO SHED TEARS
LIFE WAS SO MUCH DIFFERENT
TO THAT WHICH I HAD KNOWN
IT SEEMED TO MOVE MUCH FASTER
NOW THAT I HAD GROWN
WHEN I WAS AN OLDER MAN
I STARTED TO LOOK ROUND
AND STARTED TO APPRECIATE
MY WHOLE WORLD ALL AROUND

WHEN I BECOME AN OLD, OLD MAN
I'LL STOP AND CONTEMPLATE
ABOUT THE GOOD LIFE THAT I'VE HAD
BEFORE IT IS TOO LATE
AND THOUGH THE TIME HAS GONE TOO FAST
THE YEARS HAVE SLIPPED AWAY
I ALWAYS WILL REMEMBER
ANOTHER HAPPY DAY
WHEN I BECOME AN OLD, OLD MAN
I'LL TRY AND DO MY BEST
BEFORE IT'S TIME FOR ME TO STOP
AND TAKE MY FINAL REST

73. A CRY IN THE DARK

A SINGLE VOICE IS CRYING OUT
LONELY IN THE NIGHT
SOMEWHERE IN THE DARKNESS
HIDDEN OUT OF SIGHT
LOOKING FOR A SOMETHING
OR SOMEONE WHO WILL CARE
ANYONE OF ANY AGE
IS ANYBODY THERE
A SOUND THAT'S SO FAMILIAR
DOES ANYBODY HEAR
HEARD SO VERY OFTEN
IT COMES FROM FAR AND NEAR
WE HEAR IT IN THE NIGHT-TIME
WHEN ALL AROUND IS COLD
A SINGLE LOST AND LONELY VOICE
NOW GROWING FAINT AND OLD

74. HIDDEN FROM VIEW

BEHIND THE EYES IS HIDDEN
A WORLD YOU'LL NEVER KNOW
A PLACE WHERE THEY'LL RETREAT TO
WHERE NO ONE ELSE CAN GO
BEHIND THE EYES IS HIDDEN
THE FEELINGS THEY DON'T SHOW
LOCKED INSIDE FROM DAY TO DAY
THAT NEVER SEEM TO GO
BEHIND THE EYES IS HIDDEN
SOMETHING OUT OF VIEW
THEY REALLY WANT TO SHOW IT
BUT THEY DON'T KNOW WHAT TO DO
BEHIND THE EYES IS HIDDEN
THE TEARS THEY OFTEN CRY
HIDDEN BY THE FALSE SMILE
WHILE LIVING OUT A LIE
BEHIND THE EYES IS HIDDEN
A PERSON WE DON'T KNOW
LIVING LIFE FROM DAY TO DAY
WITH SOMETHING THAT WON'T GO
BEHIND THE EYES IS HIDDEN
IF ONLY WE COULD SEE
AND HELP THE LOST AND LONELY
TO ONE DAY JUST BE FREE

75. WHEN YOU'RE SMILING!

A SMILE CAN SHINE SO BRIGHTLY
AND LIGHTEN UP A DAY
A SPARKLE IN THE DARKEST TIMES
WITH MANY THINGS TO SAY
IT SHOWS THE WORLD SOME KINDNESS
AND SHOWS SOMEONE YOU CARE
IT SAYS THAT YOU ARE FRIENDLY
AND SAYS THAT YOU "ARE THERE!"
BUT IF YOU'RE FEELING DOWN AND LOW
AND DON'T KNOW WHAT TO DO
YOUR DAY WILL FEEL MUCH BETTER
WHEN SOMEONE SMILES AT YOU
A SMILE IS ALWAYS PRICELESS
SHARE ONE EVERY DAY
AND MAKE SOMEONE FEEL BETTER
AS YOU GO ALONG YOUR WAY

www.ingramcontent.com/pod-product-compliance
Lightning Source LLC
LaVergne TN
LVHW022112080426
835511LV00007B/776